NATIONALITY: THE ORDER OF THE DAY

THE DIVINE MESSAGE AND WARNING

ALL GARVEYITES, RASTAFARIANS,

BLACK NATIONALIST & PAN AFRICANS

BY
GRAND SHEIK BROTHER KUDJO ADWO EL
MOORISH SCIENCE TEMPLE OF AMERICA
CANAANLAND - TORONTO

EDITED BY
SIS. TAUHEEDAH S. NAJEE-ULLAH EL
MOORISH SCIENCE TEMPLE CALIFORNIA, INC.

Califa Media®
Canaanland
A Moorish Guide Publishing
Company
cmcanaanland@gmail.com

Nationality: The Order Of The Day
  The Divine Message and Warning All Garveyites, Rastafarians,
  Black Nationalist & Pan Africans

By
Grand Sheik Brother Kudjo Adwo El
Moorish Science Temple of America
Canaanland - Toronto

Edited by
Sis. Tauheedah S. Najee-Ullah El
Moorish Science Temple California, Inc.

TABLE OF CONTENTS

LIVICATION

This is livicated to my Mother, Father, Sister and Goddess, My Spiritual brother Grand Sheik Richard Neal-Bey for being spiritually aware to see my dim light and direct it home to the MST of A.

To Grand Sheik Labron C Neal Bey for your perseverance, Loyalty, Trust and Lessons given to me on the Divine and National Movement and the importance to my belonging to this Movement:

To Nat'l Grand Sheik 8126 for his Humility, Grand Sheik Temple #7 for his powerful delivery and all members and Grand body of the Prophets Temple at 8126 South Cottage Grove for the Universal Love showed to their Moorish Family from Canaanland.

To my Grand Body Asst. Grand Sheik, Sgt. Mufti, 1st and 2nd Lt. Mufti, Grand Secretary and Secretaries, Grand Chairman and ALL Canaanland Moors.

To Bro. Edward Mealy El, C.M Bey, C. Kirkman Bey, The Great Seal Moors, Moors Order of the Roundtable, R.V. Bey, Bro. Sabir Bey, Grand Sheik Taj Tarik Bey and Nature Bey for your monumental works, trials and tribulations.

To the Washitaw Nation's Prince Alim El Bey and his Royal Moabitess Khadirah Maat El Bey for giving us their time and energy whenever we need it.

To Grand Governor Amir Heru Ranesi El for being a brother and teacher in Moorish Science.

To the Vanguard of our Illustrious Prophet, Sheik Elihu Pleasant Bey for speaking of what the Prophets directions were for the movement and to All true and conscious Moorish Americans of the Divine and National Movement, True Upright Nations and Vanguards of Truth. And to the dirty moors that sold out the Prophet, IT'S TIME AND WE ARE HERE TO CLEAN OUR FATHERS HOUSE!!!!!

THE MARCUS GARVEY AND UNIA PAPERS PROJECT

MOORISH-AMERICAN PRAYER

Allah, the Father of the Universe,

The Father of Love, Truth, Peace, Freedom and Justice,

Allah is my Protector, my Guide and my Salvation by night and by day.

Through His Holy Prophet, DREW Ali.

Amen.

1

I. WORDS TO KNOW:

SOURCES

Black, H.C. *Black's Law Dictionary.* 4th. St.Paul, MN: West Publishing, 1891.

Martin, E. and Law, J., ed. *Oxford Dictionary of Law.* Oxford, UK: Oxford University, 2009.

Yogis, John. *Canadian Law Dictionary* . Hauppauge NY: Barron's Educational Series, 1990.

ADJUDICATION- *The act of giving a judicial ruling such as a judgment or decree. The term is used particularly in bankruptcy proceedings, in which the order declaring a debtor bankrupt is called adjudication*

ADMONITION- *Cautionary advice or warning*

AUTHORITY- *Permission, a right coupled with the power to do an act or order others to act. Often one person gives another authority to act, as an employer to an employee, a principal to an agent, a corporation to its officers, or governmental empowerment to perform certain functions. There are different types of authority, including "apparent authority" when a principal gives an agent various signs of authority to make others believe he or she has authority; "express authority" or "limited authority," which spells out exactly what authority is granted (usually a written set of instructions) "implied authority," which flows from the position one holds and "general authority," which is the broad power to act for another.*

AGENT- *A person who has received the power to act on behalf of another (the principal), binding that other person as if he or she were themselves making the decisions with a third-party.*

ALIEN- *An individual citizen of a state but so characterized by and while in transit, working, residing or otherwise in the territory of another state while not in receipt of any immigration status in the host state.*

ALLOCUTION- *In law means "to speak out formally."*

AMITY- *mutual understanding and a peaceful relationship, esp. between nations; peace; accord.*

AFFIDAVIT- *An affidavit is the written equivalent of giving oral evidence under oath by the "deponent", who is the person who makes the affidavit. It is a written description of facts that is sworn or solemnly declared to be true. An affidavit is usually made in the context of court proceedings. Hearsay evidence is allowed as long as the source of the deponent's information is identified, and the deponent takes an oath that he/she believes the evidence is true.*

ANNEXATION- *The act or an instance of annexing, esp. new territory, to incorporate (territory) into an existing political unit such as a country, state, county, or city, incorporation by joining or uniting.*

BLACK- *Soiled or stained, without any moral quality or goodness, dead, grotesque, morbid, or unpleasant aspects of life.*

BOND- *Written guaranty or pledge which is purchased from a bonding company or by an individual as security ("bondsman") to guarantee some form of performance, including showing up in court ("bail bond"), properly complete construction or other contract terms ("performance bond"), that the bonded party will not steal or mismanage funds, that a purchased article is the real thing, or that title is good. If there is a failure then the bonding company will make good up to the amount of the bond.*

BILL OF EXCHANGE- *A written order from one person (the payor) to another, signed by the person giving it, requiring the person to whom it is addressed to pay on demand or at some fixed future date, a certain sum of money, to either the person identified as payee or to any person presenting the bill of exchange.*

BELIEF- *A religious tenet or tenets; religious creed or faith, right without positive knowledge or proof.*

BAR ASSOCIATION- *an organization of lawyers. There are two types, one of which is official and usually called an "integrated bar," which is qualified* by the particular state's highest court to establish rules for admission and conduct. There are also local bar associations by city which are unofficial and voluntary, but do conduct the business of attorneys, such as settling fee disputes and working with the local courts on rules.

CAVEAT EMPTOR- *"Let the buyer beware" or that the buyers should examine and check for themselves things which they intend to purchase and that they cannot later hold the vendor responsible for the broken condition of the thing bought. The concept of "buyer beware" tells the potential purchaser that if it seeks greater protection than its own investigations, inspections and inquiries provide, it should seek appropriate warranties from the vendor or, if that cannot be bargained, to seek out an insurer to cover anticipated future risks.*

CODE- *A collection of written laws gathered together, usually covering specific subject matter. Federal statutes which deal with legal matters are grouped together in codes. Some codes are administrative and have the force of law even though they were created and adopted by regulatory agencies and are not actually statutes or laws.*

CHATTEL- *Moveable items of property which are neither land nor permanently attached to land or a building, either directly or vicariously through attachment to real property. The opposite of chattel is real property which includes lands or buildings. All property which is not real property is said to be chattel. "Personal property" or "personality" are other words sometimes used to describe the concept of chattel.*

CONVEYANCE- *A means of conveying, especially a vehicle for transportation.*

CONSTITUTION- *The fundamental, underlying document which establishes the government of a nation or state.*

CANADIAN MONARCHY- *A system of government in which a hereditary monarch is the sovereign of Canada, holding the position of head of state; the incumbent is Elizabeth II, officially called Queen of Canada.*

CESTUI QUE TRUST-*(properly pronounced ses-tee kay, but lawyers popularly pronounce it setty kay) from old French. 1) An old-fashioned expression for the beneficiary of a trust. 2) "The one who trusts" or the person who will benefit from the trust and will receive payments or a future distribution from the trust's assets.*

COMMERCIAL LAW- *The legal regulations governing transactions and related matters in business and trade.*

COMMON LAW- *A system of jurisprudence based on judicial precedents rather those statutory laws.*

COLOR OF LAW- *The appearance of an act being performed based upon legal right or enforcement of statute, when in reality no such right exists. An outstanding example is found in the civil rights acts which penalize law enforcement officers for violating civil rights by making arrests "under color of law" of peaceful protesters or to disrupt voter registration. It could apply to phony traffic arrests in order to raise revenue from fines or extort payoffs to forget the ticket.*

CIVIL LAW- *Civil law jurisdictions purport to provide all citizens with an accessible and written collection of the laws which apply to them and which judges must follow. Law as between citizens; law which regulates affairs between citizens or persons as between themselves.*

COURT CLERK- *An official or employee who handles the business of a court or a system of courts, maintains files of each case, and issues routine documents. Most courtrooms have a clerk to keep records and assist the judge in the management of the court.*

CONFLICT OF INTEREST- *A situation in which a person has a duty to more than one person or organization, but cannot do justice to the actual or potentially adverse interests of both parties. When a public official's personal interests are contrary to his/her loyalty to public business. An attorney, an accountant, a business adviser or realtor cannot represent two parties in a dispute and must avoid even the appearance of conflict.*

CONTRACT LAW- *Can be classified, as is habitual in civil law systems, as part of a general law of obligations, based on the Latin phrase pacta sunt servanda (pacts must be kept).*

CONTRACT- *Is a legally binding exchange of promises or agreement between parties that the law will enforce.*

COLOURED- *Having color or a certain color, artificially produced, not natural.*

COMPENSATION- *Something given or received as an equivalent for services, debt, loss, injury, suffering, lack, etc.; indemnity.*

CORPORATION *-When a Government creates a corporation, it does so by statute or by issuing a charter or a certificate, after which the corporation is, an independent legal person in the eyes of the law.*

DOMICILE- *The residence where you have your permanent home or principal establishment and to where, whenever you are absent, you intend to return; the location where an individual, partnership, or corporation establishes permanent residence as per legal obligations.*

DENATIONALIZE- *To deprive of national status, attachments, or characteristics.*

DUE PROCESS- *A fundamental principle of fairness in all legal matters, both civil and criminal, especially in the courts. All legal procedures set by statute and court practice, including notice of rights, must be followed for each individual so that no prejudicial or unequal treatment will result.*

DE FACTO- *Existing whether right or not.*

DE JURE- *The term has come to describe a total adherence of the law. Eg. DE JURE GOVERNMENT.*

DELEGATION- *Is the handing of a task over to another person, usually a subordinate. It is the assignment of authority and responsibility to another person to carry out specific activities. However the person who* *delegated the work remains accountable for the outcome of the delegate work. It allows a subordinate to make decisions.*

DURESS- *Where a person is prevented from acting (or not acting) according to their free will, by threats or force of another, it is said to be "under duress". Contracts signed under duress are voidable and, in many places, you cannot be convicted of a crime if you can prove that you were forced or threatened into committing the crime.*

EGALITARIANISM- *(derived from the French word égal, meaning equal or level) is a political doctrine that holds that all people should be treated as equals from birth. Generally it applies to being held equal under the law, the church, and society at large. In actual practice, one may be considered an egalitarian in most areas listed above, even if not subscribing to equality in every possible area of individual difference.*

EXCISE TAX- *Are taxes paid when purchases are made on a specific good, such as gasoline. Excise taxes are often included in the price of the product. There are also excise taxes on activities, such as on wagering or on highway usage by trucks.*

EMPEROR/EMPRESS- *The male/female sovereign or supreme ruler of an empire*

EMBEZZLEMENT- *The crime of stealing the funds or property of an employer, company or government or misappropriating money or assets held in trust.*

ENACTMENT- *A law or a statute; a document which is published as an enforceable set of written rules is said to be "enacted".*

EXPATRIATE- *To renounce allegiance to one's homeland, Voluntary departure from the nation of one's birth for permanent or prolonged residence in another nation.*

FIDUCIARY- *A person to whom property or power is entrusted for the benefit of another, in the nature of trust and confidence, as in public* *affairs, depending on public confidence for value or currency, as fiat money.*

FIAT MONEY- *Legal tender, especially paper currency, authorized by a government but not based on or convertible into gold or silver.*

FAITH- *A system of religious belief, Confident belief in the truth, value, or trustworthiness of a person, idea, or thing.*

FRUITION- *Attainment of anything desired; realization; accomplishment, Enjoyment derived from use or possession, something that is made real or concrete.*

G.O.D- Government Ordinance Department.

GRANTOR- *The party who transfers title in real property (seller, giver) to another (buyer, recipient) by grant deed or quitclaim deed.*

IN PROPRIA PERSONA- *Latin "for one's self," acting on one's own behalf, generally used to identify a person who is acting as his/her own attorney in a lawsuit.*

INCOME- *The monetary payment received for goods or services, or from other sources, as rents or investments.*

JURISDICTION- *Refers to a court's authority to judge over a situation usually acquired in one of three ways: over acts committed in a defined territory, over certain types of cases, or over certain persons.*

JUDICIAL- *Pertaining to judgment in courts of justice or to the administration of justice, pertaining to courts of law or to judges; judiciary, of or pertaining to a judge; proper to the character of a judge, giving or seeking judgment, as in a dispute or contest; determinative.*

LEGISLATURE- *A deliberative body of persons, usually elective, who are empowered to make, change, or repeal the laws of a country or state; the branch of government having the power to make laws, as distinguished from the executive and judicial branches of government.*

LIEN- *Any official claim or charge against property or funds for payment of a debt or an amount owed for services rendered. A lien is usually a formal document signed by the party to whom money is owed and sometimes by the debtor who agrees to the amount due. A lien carries with it the right to sell property, if necessary, to obtain the money.*

LICENSE- *Governmental permission to perform a particular act (like getting married), conduct a particular business or occupation, operate machinery or vehicles after proving ability to do so safely or use property for a certain purpose.*

LABEL- *A short word or phrase descriptive of a person, group, intellectual movement, etc. a word or phrase indicating that what follows belongs in a particular category or classification, a brand or trademark, to put in a certain class.*

LAW- *Any system of regulations to govern the conduct of the people of a community, society or nation, in response to the need for regularity, consistency and justice based upon collective human experience.*

LETTERS PATENT- *Are a type of legal instrument in the form of an open letter issued by a monarch or government, granting an office, right, monopoly, title, or status to a person or to some entity such as a corporation. The opposite of letters patent is letters close which are personal in nature and sealed so that only the recipient can read their contents.*

MISNOMER- *A misapplied or inappropriate name or designation, an error in naming a person or thing.*

MOOR- *Were a mixture of various shades of diverse groups comprising East Africans, North Africans, West Africans, and Sub-Saharan Africans, comes from the Greek word mauros, meaning "black" or "very dark", an ethnic group inhabiting Republic of Mauritania and parts of Morocco, Western Sahara, Algeria, Niger and Mali.*

NATIONAL- *A citizen or subject of a particular Nation who is entitled to its protection, characteristic of a people of a nation.*

NATIONALITY- *The status of belonging to a particular nation, whether by birth or naturalization, existence as a distinct nation, a nation of people, a people having / common origins or traditions and often constituting a nation, national independence, nationalism.*

NATIONALISM- *Devotion and loyalty to one's own nation, the desire for national advancement or independence, the belief that nations will benefit from acting independently rather than collectively, emphasizing national rather than international goals, the doctrine that your national culture and interests are superior to any other.*

NATURAL LAW- *A principle or body of laws considered as derived from nature, right reason, or religion and as ethically binding in human society.*

NOTARY PUBLIC- *A person authorized by the state in which the person resides to administer oaths (swearing to truth of a statement), take acknowledgments, certify documents and to take depositions if the notary is also a court reporter. The signature and seal or stamp of a notary public is necessary to attest to the oath of truth of a person making an affidavit and to attest that a person has acknowledged that he/she executed a deed, power of attorney or other document, and is required for recording in public records.*

NOTWITHSTANDING- *In spite of, even if, without regard to or impediment by other things as stated.*

PLEBISCITE- *A vote in which a population exercises the right of national self-determination.*

NEGRO- *<zoology> Any one of the Quadrumana (A division of the Primates), including apes, baboons, one of a race of black or very dark persons who inhabit the greater part of tropical Africa, and are distinguished by crisped or curly hair, flat noses, and thick protruding* *lips; also, any black person of unmixed African blood, wherever found. A river rising in central Argentina and flowing about 644 km (400 mi) eastward to the Atlantic Ocean. A river rising in southern Brazil and flowing about 805 km (500 mi) generally southwest to the Uruguay River in central Uruguay. A river of northwest South America flowing about 2,253 km (1,400 mi) from eastern Colombia to the Amazon River near Manaus, Brazil. Part of its course forms a section of the Colombia-Venezuela border.*

OFFICIAL- *A public officer or governmental employee who is empowered to exercise judgment. 3) n. an officer of a corporation or business.*

ORDINANCE- *An executive decision of a government which has not been subjected to a legislative assembly (contrary to a statute). It is often detailed and not, as would be a statute, of general wording or application. This term is in disuse in many jurisdictions and the words "regulations" or "bylaws" are preferred.*

PERSON- *Law. A human being (natural person) or a group of human beings, a corporation, a partnership, an estate, or other legal entity (artificial person or juristic person) recognized by law as having rights and duties.*

PUBLIC- *The people of the nation, state, county, district or municipality which the government serves. 2) adj. referring to any agency, interest, property, or activity which is under the authority of the government or which belongs to the people. This distinguishes public from private interests as with public and private schools, public and private utilities, public and private hospitals, public and private lands and public and private roads. 3) Traded publicly via a stock market.*

PRIVATE- *Not accessible by the public, not done in the view of or with the possibility of disturbance by others.*

PSEUDO- *Not actually but having the appearance of; pretended; false or spurious; sham.*

PECU.N.I.A.RY- *M L. pecU.N.I.A.rius "pertaining to money," from pecU.N.I.A. "money, property, wealth."*

PRIVILEGE- *Etymologically "private law" or law relating to a specific individual—is a special entitlement or immunity granted by a government or other authority to a restricted group, either by birth or on a conditional basis. A privilege can be revoked in some cases. In modern democracies, a privilege is conditional and granted only after birth. By contrast, a right is an inherent, irrevocable entitlement held by all citizens or all human beings from birth.*

PRIVY COUNCIL- *Is a body that advises the head of state of a nation, typically in a monarchy. The word "privy" means "private" or "secret" thus a privy council was originally a committee of the monarch's closest advisors to give confidential advice on affairs of state.*

QUESI JUDICIAL- *Refers to decisions made by administrative tribunals or government officials to which the rules of natural justice apply. In judicial decisions, the principles of natural justice always apply. But between routine government policy decisions and the traditional court forums lies a hybrid form of rights of a person.*

ROYAL CANADIAN MINT- *Produces all of Canada's circulation coins, and manufactures circulation coins on behalf of other nations. The RCM is a Crown Corporation that operates under the legislative basis of the Royal Canadian Mint Act.*

RIGHT- *An entitlement to something, whether to concepts like justice and due process or to ownership of property or some interest in property, real or personal. These rights include: various freedoms; protection against interference with enjoyment of life and property; civil rights enjoyed by citizens such as voting and access to the courts; natural rights accepted by civilized societies; human rights to protect people throughout the world from terror, torture, barbaric practices and deprivation of civil rights and profit from their labor; and such constitutional guarantees as the right to* *freedoms of speech, press, religion, assembly and petition. 2) adj. just, fair, correct.*

REVOCATION- *Nullification or withdrawal, esp. of an offer to contract, the state of being cancelled or annulled.*

SOVEREIGNTY- *The quality or state of being sovereign, the status, dominion, power or authority of a sovereign, complete independence and self-government, government free from external control.*

SOVEREIGN- *A group or body of persons or a state having sovereign authority, belonging to or characteristic of a sovereign or sovereignty; royal, being above all others in character, importance, excellence, a king, queen, or other noble person who serves as chief of state; a ruler or monarch.*

STATUTE- *A law enacted by a legislature. There are also statutes which are not codified.*

STATUTORY- *Prescribed or authorized by or punishable under a statute.*

STATUTORY LAW- *Written law (as opposed to oral or customary law) set down by a legislature or other governing authority such as the executive branch of government in response to a perceived need to clarify the functioning of government, improve civil order, answer a public need, to codify existing law, or for an individual or company to obtain special treatment.*

SUIT- *Generic term for any filing of a complaint (or petition) asking for legal redress by judicial action, often called a "lawsuit.*

USURPATION- *To take power, wrongfully or by force.*

USURY- *Lending money at extensive rates of interest.*

VENUE- *The place of a crime or cause of action, the designation, in the pleading, of the jurisdiction where a trial will be held, the designation, in the pleading, of the jurisdiction where a trial will be held.*

WARD- *A person (usually a minor) who has a guardian appointed by the court to care for and take responsibility for that person.*

"Application of higher knowledge is the key to open the mental slave lock." (Garvey 1978)

"In these modern days there came a forerunner, who was divinely prepared by the great GOD-Allah and his name is Marcus Garvey." (Noble Drew Ali 1928).

THE MARCUS GARVEY AND UNIA PAPERS PROJECT

II. MARCUS MOSIAH GARVEY II

August 17, 1887 - Whirlwind

"My enemies in America have done much to hold me up to public contempt and ridicule, but have failed. They believe that the only resort is to stir up national prejudice against me, in that I was not born within the borders of the United States of America.

"I am not in the least concerned about such propaganda, because I have traveled the length and breadth of America and I have discovered that among the fifteen million of my race, only those who have exploited and lived off the ignorance of the masses are concerned with where I was born. The masses of the people are looking for leadership; they desire sincere, honest guidance in racial affairs. As proof of this I may mention, that the largest number of members in the Universal Negro Improvement Association (of which I am President-General) are to be found in America, and are native born Americans. I know these people so well and I love them so well, that I would not for one minute think that they would fall for such an insidious propaganda." (Garvey 1978)

Who was this illustrious being sent with a Divine message to the people called the Negro, Colored, Blacks, African American/Canadian and other misnomers?

His name is Marcus Garvey to the world, but to those who identify Melanin beings as Gods and Goddesses in fleshly form, he is The Honorable Messiah Marcus Garvey. In a general sense, a MESSIAH means any such savior and liberator of the world. A savior is one who helps people achieve salvation, or saves them from something. The prefix Honorable is a title of quality attached to the names of certain classes of persons. When Marcus Garvey founded and became leader of the Universal Negro Improvement Association (U.N.I.A) and the African Communities League (A.C.L.) in 1914, he claimed the title "The Honorable." This is customary when one privatizes an organization as part of a Masonic or religious movement. In the prior quote from our Messiah, there are words that are taken for granted instead of innerstood as a hidden message to be received so that they may be saved. The first important term is Nation. Garvey states that National prejudice was the weapon used against him. Who is the National showing prejudice to Marcus Garvey? National is an adjective which relates to, belonging to, representing, or affecting a nation, especially a nation as a whole rather than a part of it or section of its territory.

Prejudice in this case is described as an unfounded hatred, fear, or mistrust of a person or group, especially one of a particular religion, ethnicity, nationality, sexual preference, or social status, to cause harm or disadvantage to somebody or something or to make somebody form an opinion about somebody or something in advance, especially an irrational one, based on insufficient knowledge. It is easy to see, when we break things down to a minute level, how the European thinks. By making a Nation of a people hold prejudice against an individual of that same Nation, speaking out for the disadvantages experienced and insperienced by that Nation, it causes the Savior to be martyred and keeps the initiator of the martyrdom safe from prosecution. Messiah Garvey knew that the Order of the Day for European Supremacy was melanin separation.

"Another example of black attraction to violent anti-white and anti-Semitic hatemongering came in 1914, when Marcus Garvey, a Jamaican immigrant, formed the Universal Negro Improvement Association (U.N.I.A.), a pro-Nazi black racist cult. The images are of newspaper advertisements for Garvey enterprises; one crude cartoon shows Garvey employing black labor, another illustration depicts a black mother and child threatened by a burning cross, and the "Let's Put It Over" advertisement encourages the immigration by American blacks to Liberia. Another Garvey effort which

unfortunately met with very limited success. Black racist con artist Marcus Garvey, whose venomous Jew-hatred and America-hatred led him to support Hitler in the 1930s. Garvey, in the plumes, shared the taste of many other black leaders for outlandish costumes and ostentatious display." (Jewish Task Force 2004).

The purpose of the J.T.F. is to spread propaganda implicating Islam as a terrorist religion. So the next common sense question would be, why Marcus Garvey? He wasn't Muslim...was he?

Marcus Messiah Garvey knew that his Divine purpose was to liberate and unite "Africans" at home and abroad; to think as a Nation, sufficient for self based on a legacy that predated the ones that had us in mental and physical, now spiritual slavery. Garvey's position was that, no matter what flag we decide to live under, no matter the constitution and laws that govern that flag, the government it represented was set up with no intention of benefiting the "colored" person. Marcus Garvey the Messiah stated "we can expect very little from the efforts of present-day statesmen of other races, in that their plans are laid only in the interests of their own people and not in the interest of Negroes", which tells us he understood that from a national perspective, separated, we had no rights as "Negroes" unless UNITED as a NATION. As we become more dependent on the slave master for our survival, we slowly die from anticipating food for a stomach empty too long.

Our Messiahs philosophies regarding Black Nationalism were so profound that they become known as the study of Garveyism, whose focus is the complete, total and never ending redemption of the continent of Africa by people of African ancestry, at home and abroad. It is rooted in one basic idea: "whatsoever things common to man that man has done, man can do". Therefore, Africa can become as glorious and profoundly advanced in the scientific and technological realm as any, when "Africans" will it to be. The guidelines of Garveyism are 1) race first 2) self-reliance and 3) NATIONhood. The ultimate goal of Garveyism is a United States of Africa which will protect the interests of "Black" people worldwide. Marcus Messiah Garvey was more than a pan African, even if he didn't think so himself. The majority of his followers took the title Messiah for granted. His purpose was to unite his people through their nationality as—what he understood at that time—African.

The Messiah considered what European Americans did to the "Negro" a crime to the "Black" race and called for a united front against the disenfranchisement, lynching's and utter disrespect for the race as a whole. Messiah Marcus Garvey visited Toronto in 1924 to establish a branch of the Universal Negro Improvement Association (U.N.I.A.). Barred from entering the United States, Garvey attempted to implement his program in Montreal and in Hamilton. During October 1928 he attempted to visit U.N.I.A. branches in the U.S., but was blocked by immigration authorities. In 1937, however, he was principal of a summer school of African philosophy and held a regional U.N.I.A. conference in Toronto, and visited Nova Scotia and New Brunswick. In 1938, Garvey attended the U.N.I.A.'s eighth international convention in Toronto. Malcolm X's father Earl Little, and mother, Louise, met at a U.N.I.A. convention in Montreal, Canada. Both were influenced by Garvey's doctrines and the U.N.I.A.. Why would the Messiah even consider Canadian cities, in particular Nova Scotia, Montreal and Toronto, as sites to establish chapters of the U.N.I.A. and then embark on promotional tours? Because he overstood that the influx of migrants to Canada at that time Caribbean, and those migrating to Toronto came mainly from his homeland; Jamaica. This clearly attests to his determination to unite his people "at home and abroad".

"Where did the name of the organization come from? It was while speaking to a West Indian Negro who was a passenger with me from Southampton, who was returning home to the West Indies from Basutoland with his Basuto

wife, that I further learned of the horrors of native life in Africa. He related to me in conversation such horrible and pitiable tales that my heart bled within me. Retiring from the conversation to my cabin, all day and the following night I pondered over the subject matter of that conversation, and at midnight, lying flat on my back, the vision and thought came to me that I should name the organization the Universal Negro Improvement Association and African Communities (Imperial) League. Such a name I thought would embrace the purpose of all black humanity. Thus to the world a name was born, a movement created, and a man became known." (Garvey 1978).

The U.N.I.A.'s Declaration of Rights were adopted in the 1920's, marking the evolution of the movement into a black nationalist one. Also, by a unanimous vote, Garvey was elected provisional president of Africa and the official colors of the movement, Red, Black, and Green were endorsed. The U.N.I.A. red, black, and green flag has been adopted as the Black Liberation Flag. The symbolism of these colors is explained in the song *Rally Round*, by Steel Pulse.

> *Marcus say - Sir Marcus say*
> *Red for the Blood*
> *That flowed like the river*
> *Marcus say - Sir Marcus say*
> *Green for the land Africa*
> *Marcus say*
> *Yellow for the Gold*
> *That they stole*
> *Sir Marcus say*
> *Black for the people*
> *It was looted from*

The preamble of the 1929 constitution states that the U.N.I.A. is a *"social, friendly, humanitarian, charitable, educational, institutional, constructive and expansive society, and is founded by persons desiring to the utmost to work for the general upliftment of the people of African ancestry of the world. And the members pledge themselves to do all in their power to conserve the rights of their noble race* and to respect the rights of all mankind, believing always in the Brotherhood of Man and the Fatherhood of God." In early 1922, he went to Atlanta, Georgia, for a meeting with Edward Young Clarke, KKK imperial giant. Messiah Garvey said of the meeting:

> "I regard the Klan, the Anglo-Saxon clubs and White American societies, as far as the Negro is concerned, as better friends of the race than all other groups of hypocritical whites put together. I like honesty and fair play. You may call me a Klansman if you will, but, potentially, every white man is a Klansman. As far as the Negro in competition with whites socially, economically and politically is concerned, there is no use lying." (Garvey 1978).

Marcus Messiah Garvey was a strong on his views regarding self-sufficiency and race pride. He taught that we are today what our foremothers and forefathers were and that the immaculate history behind us is our legacy to carry on to the end of times. Marcus Garvey knew that through propaganda by Europeans, many that belong to the Nation that civilized mankind would leave civilization to join the race of barbarians.

"The world is indebted to us for the benefits of civilization. They stole our arts and sciences...so why should we be ashamed of ourselves?" Hon. Marcus Garvey

Our Messiah never spoke mildly of African cowardice and traitors and pointed out those who he considered sellouts to his race who refused to contribute to the momentum of our glorious Legacy. For instance, Messiah Marcus Garvey suspected that W. E. Du Bois was prejudiced against him because he was a Caribbean native with dark skin. By the late 1920s, Du Bois's antagonism had turned to almost pathological disdain. To him, Garvey was "a lunatic or a traitor." Garvey called Du Bois "purely and simply a white man's nigger" and "a little Dutch, a little French, a little Negro ... a mulatto ... a monstrosity." This led to a bitter relationship between Garvey and the NAACP. Garvey would later accuse Du Bois of paying conspirators to sabotage the Black Star Line and destroy his reputation. Du Bois was, nevertheless, a strong supporter of Pan-Africanism. The movement that our Messiah started has influenced many people from all walks of life to embrace and express his name as a form of respect. Martin Luther King said once in a speech that Garvey "was the first man of color to lead and develop a mass movement. He was the first man on a mass scale and level to give millions of Negroes a sense of dignity and destiny. And make the Negro feel he was somebody." King was also the recipient of the first Marcus Garvey Prize for Human Rights on December 10, 1968 issued by the Jamaican Government and presented to King's widow.

III. Influential Members of the U.N.I.A.

Rabbi Arnold Josiah Ford
April 23 1877—September 16 1935

The first "Black" Rabbi in America, and a prominent member of Harlem's "Black Jews". Rabbi Arnold Josiah Ford was composer of many U.N.I.A songs. He co-authored *The Universal Ethiopian Anthem* with Benjamin E. Burrell and officially functioned as director of U.N.I.A Band, Orchestra Band of the African Legion and the Liberty Hall Choir. He was a luminary in the U.N.I.A. Ford offered Hebrew language and religious instruction to a number of laypeople and clergy in the Harlem area. Ford worked with both Mathew's Commandment Keepers Congregation and the Moorish Zionist Congregation led by Mordecai Herman in the 1920's. In 1930, Rabbi Ford and a small group of "Black Jews" went to Ethiopia where they participated in the coronation of Emperor Haile Selassie, created a school, and acquired 800 acres of land for the purpose of uniting "Black Jews" of the Diaspora with their brothers already in Ethiopia. He died there in 1935.

Wentworth Arthur Matthew
June 23, 1892—December 1973

Founder of the Commandment Keepers Congregation, Mathew was influenced by European Jews he met at the U.N.I.A., in particular, when he learned about Beta Israel. His congregation is featured in a scene from the 1970 motion picture *The Angel Levine,* starring Harry Belafonte.

"The Negro is crying out for a Mohammad, a Prophet who will bring him the Koran of economic and intelligent welfare."– Marcus Garvey

IV. INFLUENCED BY MARCUS GARVEY

Formed by MCs Yasiin Bey (f.k.a. Mos Def) and Talib Kweli, the rap group Black Star and their self-titled debut album reference the shipping line founded by Messiah Marcus Garvey.

In "Halftime" off the *Illmatic* album, Nas says, "And in the darkness/ I'm heartless/ like when the narcs hit/ word to Marcus Garvey".

Revolutionary hip hop group Dead Prez refer to Marcus Garvey in many of their songs and live by his Red, Black and Green philosophy. RBG is variously described and one description is "Read Bout Garvey".

Sellout rapper Ludacris, in his popular video "Pimpin All over the World", disrespects the legacy of our Messiah by wearing a T-Shirt with: "*A people without the knowledge of their past history, origin and culture is like a tree without roots,*" a quote attributed to Marcus Garvey.

Kwame Nkrumah named the national shipping line of Ghana the Black Star Line in honor of Garvey and the U.N.I.A. and also named the national soccer team the Black Stars.

We hear too much and have to many examples of what our Messiah did for us but where did he find the drive to stand up and speak, with an activated Crown and Throat chakra, in favour of all Melanin people worldwide? Our Messiah too had an inspirational person he found worthy to learn from, and, as Garvey was a powerhouse in his own right, how powerful was his inspiration?

V. Influenced Marcus Garvey

Booker T. Washington

"No greater injury can be done to any youth than to let him feel that because he belongs to this or that race he will be advanced in life regardless of his own merits or efforts."

"We must reinforce argument with results"

As a slave child, Booker T Washington knew that he was entitled to rights just as much as any other person. What must be made note of is that he was a mixed child, whose features favoured the mothers' strong Melanin genes. What must also be made note of is that his father was a European from a nearby farm, and his mother was a cook—let's just say a slave, also. (Today we see that many Melanin men have taken up the role of the European from the nearby farm.) This Melanin being was founder of Tuskegee Institute in 1881. He built on a foundation of self-reliance due to his slave childhood.

From some things that I have said one may get the idea that some of the slaves did not want freedom. This is not true. I have never seen one who did not want to be free, or one who would return to slavery."- Booker T. Washington

Washington was emancipated at the age of nine (9), the number of completion in Divine Mathematics. He was destined to be a supporter of Melanin beings and influence race relations. He was supported by many European elitist including John D. Rockefeller which in my opinion was a form of subliminal reparations. The majority of Europeans, whether citizen or elite, had a spoon in the slavery pot. Having a European father, and knowing that he was a bastard child was his drive to be something more than society perceived him to be. His motto was self-discipline, hard work and education in order for melanin beings to obtain their respect.

While this leader's effect inspired him to found the U.N.I.A. Messiah Garvey encountered another Moor influential inspiration when he traveled to England in 1912. There he worked with the publication African Times and Orient review and where was first introduced to writings by Booker T Washington

Duse Mohammed Ali

A Moorish National born in 1866, Duse Mohammad Ali was an actor, historian, journalist, editor, lecturer, traveler, and publisher. Through his political and cultural journals he advocated Pan African-Asian Nationalism. This forum for African intellectuals and activists from around the world drew the attention of a wide variety of contributors. Besides Ali's strong Nationalist and Pan Africanist views, he was an active follower of Islam, having in 1926 established the Universal Islamic Society in Detroit, Michigan. Duse Ali had a thorough understanding of Moorish history displayed in 1902 when he produced Othello and the Merchant of Venice at Hull Yorkshire, playing the parts of Othello and the Prince of Morocco, respectively. To validate this, Yorkshire has a strong symbolic meaning because of the Yorkshire Moors. Duse Mohammed Ali's organization was the precursor to Noble Drew Ali's Moorish Science Temple.

African Times and Orient Review

Contributors to the *African Times* and *Orient Review* included such notables as George Bernard Shaw, Lord Litton, Annie Besant, Sir Harry H. Johnston, William H Ferris and Marcus Garvey. Copies were circulated in Egypt, West Africa, England, Japan, British Guiana, the United States, Australia, Canada, Hindustan (India), Ceylon (Sri Lanka), Jamaica and Nigeria. The "Islamic" influence can be seen in Marcus Garvey's motto "One God One Aim One Destiny" which originated with Duse Ali's Universal Islamic Society. In the U.N.I.A., the motto was preceded by "May our Rights proclaim, in the most sacred name Allah". Ali's social and academic commitments were vibratory, being seen not only in our Messiah Garvey and his vision but also in those visions of the Prophet Noble Drew Ali and the Messenger Elijah Muhammad. Every major influential Asiatic that Duse Ali came in contact with started a newspaper which became his passion. He strongly trusted in the circulation of our newspapers to educate and inform our masses: the U.N.I.A had the *Negro World*, the M.S.T of A had the *Moorish Guide* and the N.O.I had *Muhammad Speaks*

"All these newspapers were used to build financial foundation and to also market themselves to the public. The *Moorish Guide* was distributed in more than 15 states from 1926 to 1928." moorsgate.com

VI. The Black man's God according to Messiah Garvey

"Look to Africa, when a black king shall be crowned for the day of deliverance is at hand!" – Messiah Garvey

Marcus Messiah Garvey is the one that recognized Haile Selassie as a coming Christ for Melanin beings. Rastas consider Marcus Garvey a Prophet, a reincarnation of John the Baptist because of his statements telling "Blacks" to look to Africa for the Black God. Marcus Garvey knew that liberation came when we realized who we were as a people and that our legacy existed before us and that we belonged forever to it

> *"I know no national boundary where the Negro is concerned. The whole world is my province until Africa is free"–Messiah Garvey*

> *"To me, a man has no master but God. Man in his authority is a sovereign lord. As for the individual man, so of the individual race. This feeling makes man so courageous, so bold, as to make it impossible for his brother to intrude upon his rights. So few of us can understand what it takes to make a man—the man who will never say die; the man who will never give up; the man who will never depend upon others to do for him what he ought to do for himself; the man who will not blame God, who will not blame Nature, who will not blame Fate for his condition; but the man who will go out and make conditions to suit himself."— (Garvey 1978).*

> *"Any leadership that teaches to depend on another race is a race that will enslave you. We need a leadership of our own to make us FREEMEN"* (Garvey 1978).

> *"We must canonize our own Saints"* - (Garvey 1978).

Messiah Garvey was a clairvoyant, a Magi that channeled and he was one who might or might not have really realized his full prophesy. Garvey states in *Philosophies and Opinions of Marcus Garvey* (1978) that the God we as melanin beings worship and adore is a God of Peace (ISLAM) and War. He goes on to say that the greatest battle was not between man and man, but Almighty God (Higher-self) and Lucifer (Lower-self). This is the Hermetic axiom as above, so below, as within, so without of the Universal Law of Correspondence. He had enough of an overstanding to know that when Evil comes with his Army, so will the All Righteous come with an army to overthrow those trying to go against Natural Law.

"God is really on the side of the strongest peoples because God made all men equal and He never gave superior power to anyone class or group of people over another, and anyone who can get the advantage over another is pleasing God, because that is the servant who has taken care of God's command in exercising authority over the world." Messiah Marcus Garvey

Our Messiah knew that we were subliminally fooled into having our God in an image unlike our own. Due to the propaganda against Africa and anything dark, we accepted the fact that we were a sinned people and gave up our birthright as the founders of civilization, diverting to the status of servants to civilization. He knew that the yellow man had a God in his image, the European had a God in his image, and if we were going to be free thinkers, we had to have and recognize that we had our own God, and didn't need to go piggy backing blessings from a God not in our image.

"We have prayed to God (Haile Selassie) for vision and for leadership and he has given us a UNIVERSAL VISION"- Hon Marcus Garvey

EMPEROR HAILE SELASSIE 1ST AND EMPRESS MENEN

"We must become something we have never been and for which our education and experience and environment have ill-prepared us." *(Selassie I 1966)*

Arising from Biblical prophecy partly based on Selassie's status as the only Ancient Monarch of a fully independent state, and his titles of King of Kings, Lord of Lords, and Conquering Lion of Judah (Revelation 5:5), Our Messiah was inspired, prophesized and witnessed the coming of his prophesy as Haile Selassie, God incarnate for Melanin beings. Empress Menen and Emperor Haile Selassie I, whom some of the Rastafarians call Jah, was crowned "Negus Negast (King of Kings), Elect of God, and Conquering Lion of the Tribe of Judah" in Addis Ababa on November 2, 1930. Empress Menen was crowned Nigiste Negast meaning Queen of Kings.

Here is dynamic new understanding of the real origin of the famous Eighteenth Dynasty of ancient Kemet and Kush, and the origin of the long line of kings which have ruled in Kush until Haile Selassie and Empress Menen.

Emperor Haile Selassie was named Time's Person of the Year in 1935 and the first African person to appear on the cover.

31

Ethiopia was the only African country to escape colonialism, and Haile Selassie was one of the few only National leaders accepted among the kings and queens of Nations of the World. Rastas view him with immaculate reverence and show extreme loyalty to the King of Kings, Lord of Lords.

Ras is the highest noble by Princes of the Solomonic bloodline. One had to be elevated to the rank of Negus by Imperial decree, but Ras was hereditary. Pope Pius XI gave Mussolini orders to invade Ethiopia because in 1930, he, the Pope of Rome had to attend the great coronation and bow down on his face to the Supreme Spiritual Head of the Earth Emperor Haile Selassie I, Negus Negast, Lord of Lords, Conquering Lion from the Tribe of Judah, Elect of God, Light of this World and Empress Menen, Negiste Negast. That was an ego crusher, so the Pope blessed Mussolini and ordered him to invade Ethiopia. The Pope gave Mussolini orders to invade Ethiopia as a spiritual payback, physically, for him having to bow before all nations to the Melanin God. As a member of the League of Nations, Selassie had to go before his European allies to convince them to assemble together and fight Rome and make them leave his country. He did not take the role of a coward. King Selassie I defeated Mussolini and Rome, reclaiming his Kingdom from the fascist invaders. The King James Version of the Bible plainly states in Acts 2:29-30, God made a promise to King David that of the fruit of his loins, according to the flesh, that he would raise up Christ to sit on King David's throne.

"The Prophet himself instructed his followers to respect and protect Ethiopians. In 615, Muhammad's wife and cousin sought refuge at Axum (Aksum) with a number of these followers. This group was fleeing from Mecca's leading tribe, the reactionary Kuraysh, who sent emissaries to bring them back to Arabia, but the Negus Armah protected them. An influx of immigrants and traders from Oman and Yemen during the following centuries increased the number of Muslims in Somalia, Eritrea and what is now Ethiopia. In the coastal areas, Islamic law gradually took root, and by the fourteenth century it was the basis for the official juridical code of some regions. This reflected political realities; most of the

32

inhabitants of these eastern regions were now Muslims. Their coexistence with Christianity was not always an easy one, and the sultans who ruled over parts of Ethiopian territory sometimes came into open conflict with the Christian kings. Yet, historians generally agree that the Muslim

sultans in Ethiopia were tolerant of their Christian subjects; forced conversions were rare." (Abyssinia Forever n.d.)

We must see that all applies to our liberation. We must come to a Universal ideal when it comes to Melanin beings and Freedom. Haile Selassie is the Redeemer for us all, whether in a physical sense or spiritual essence. Recognize the Glory and Goodness of our Imperial Majesties, referring to Negus Negast (King of Kings) Haile Selassie I and his consort Empress Menen, who carries the title Nigiste Negast, which means Queen of Kings.

"Ethiopia has existed for 3,000 years. In fact, it exists ever since the first man appeared on Earth. My dynasty has ruled since the Queen of Sheba met King Solomon and a Son was born of their union. It is a Dynasty that has gone thru the centuries and will go on for centuries more."—H.I.M. Haile Selassie I

The very name "Hatshepsut" itself may prove the fact that this famous Queen, who visited the land of Punt, the "Divine Land," and who built a temple on the banks of the Nile at Thebes in Upper Egypt patterned after Solomon's Temple in Jerusalem, was indeed the Queen of Sheba. "Ha," in Hebrew, means "the." Thus her actual name is "Shep," but nominatives are often interchangeable, and it could be rendered "Sheb," that is, SHEBA --"Sut is a word in Kemetic that means dark, or black. In Ages of Chaos, by Immanuel Velikovsky, he states about HETSHEPSUT, "Thy name reaches as far as the circuit of heaven, the fame of MAKERE encircles the sea". Makere is clearly the same name as Makeda, the Ethiopian name for the Queen of Sheba or Saba. The term "Sheba" or "Saba" refers to the name of the famous Ethiopian royal city at the Nile and two other Ethiopian rivers, at the upper reaches of the Nile. The Queen of Sheba is Hatshepsut, her Egyptian name, or Makeda, her Ethiopian name. He inherited his imperial blood

through his paternal grandmother, Princess Tenagnework Sahle Selassie, who was an aunt of Emperor Menelik II, and as such, claimed to be a direct descendant of Makeda.

"Her Imperial Majesty, Empress Menen being crowned on the same day as Empress implies she is not a Queen. Grimm's Law Dictionary defines Queen as whore. Though she has a King, she is setting the Empress standard from this day forth. The Queen represents the Harlot, Queen Elizabitch, riding the Beast called the British Monarchy (Rev 17:1-Rev 17:14), which has fought for the Imperial Scepter and the riches of Ethiopia through enormous deceitful tactics to claim the birthright of Africa's only un-colonized country". There is physically only one Haile Selassie and Empress Menen, but spiritually we are all Elects of God, Conquering Lions from 1 of the 12 Tribes of Isis, Ra and EL, Lights of this World which, "this world", is the mind, activated by wearing the Triple

Crown or raising to the Crown Chakra, riding the Feminine Kundalini Energy through the gates of Zion." (McLetchie El 2011).

Emperor Haile Selassie is hailed as the greatest of modern Monarchs and a symbol of the continent's vast potential. To the Garveyites and Pan Africanist, Haile Selassie I is a hero, a HERU (Light of this World). To the Rastafarians as he is the Living God incarnate, the Living perpendicular in Flesh. 2 Angels support the throne of Solomon on the Solomonic Crest. The angel to the left bears the Imperial Scepter (His Imperial Majesty) and the one on the right bears the Sword of State and Scales of Justice (MAAT, Goddess Menen). In the *Promised Key*, Leonard Percival Howell writes "King Alpha and Queen Omega said they are the Black Arc Sovereign of Most High times. If Rastafarians KNEW about Nationality, they will SEE CLEARLY, that H.I.M IS NOT GOD but God's Dignitary on the Earth plane, a living example of how we should deal with Nations of Earth. H.I.M was a Modern Noble Drew Ali.

"Our Armageddon is past. Africa has been reborn as a free continent and Africans have been reborn as free men"—H.I.M Haile Selassie I

"Africans are in bondage today because they approach spirituality through religion provided by foreign invaders and conquerors. We must stop confusing religion and spirituality. Religion is a set of rules, regulations and rituals created by humans, which were supposed to help people to grow spiritually. Due to human imperfection, religion has become corrupt, political, and divisive and a tool for power struggle. Spirituality is not theology or ideology. It is simply a Way of life, pure and original as was given by the Most High of Creation. Spirituality is a network linking us to the Most High, the universe and each other. As the essence of our existence, it embodies our culture, true identity, nationhood and destiny. A people without a nation that they can really call their own, are a people without a soul. Africa is our nation and is in spiritual and physical bondage because her leaders are turning to outside forces for solutions to African problems when everything Africa needs

35

is within her. When African righteous people come together, the world will come together. This is our divine destiny!"— Emperor Haile Selassie I.

"The young Dejazmach found himself sent to further his education, and enrolled in the new Menilek School which was founded in the city and put in charge of by an Egyptian Hanna Bey Saleb". So we know as Dejazmach, Ras Tafari was learned in the way of Moorish Egyptian Mystery Sciences. The Lion of Judah metaphysically represents the courage to enter fearlessly into the overcoming life and understanding of all things. To understand is to go under the foundation to get a good look at what's going on. Judah also represents the spiritual faculty that corresponds to the accumulation or increase in mental. Negus Negas relates to the Serpent Kings. These are the same 7 serpents around Buddha, 7 Cobras of Goddess Lakshmi, the dragons in front of Shaolin Temples, the snakes St. Patrick chased out of Ireland and the Garden of Eden's serpent. Negas were Africans enlightened by the serpentine fire or kundalini energy. This is the same serpent pharaohs had on their crowns." (McLetchie El 2011).

"And we can look on what he has done as Rastas and see a certain Christ-ness that is what we are searching for. Not as we were taught it, because first of all, to really understand what the Rastaman is saying about Haile Selassie, you haffe go move Jesus out of your mind. This idea, this Jesus concept that was given to us by Rome, you have to totally wipe it out and this God mentality, this God-consciousness. You have to move that out now and reshape it. You have to look within man not in the sky. And I think that is what a whole heap of Jamaicans find difficult. That when the Rastaman say Haile Selassie, he is trying to put what he sees in his mind about God with what we is talking about this Man. And not knowing that what he sees in his

mind is what is in man. There is no other concept outside of man. Is man make God. If there was no man, there wouldn't be any concept of God. So you have to look within man to find the reality of life and what life really means.

So when the Rastaman says Haile Selassie, because man cannot see man as the Supreme Being. Him trying to look outside of himself fe that consciousness. And the Rastaman is saying, no, that consciousness is here" (Van Pelt 1998).

The Dynasty of Ethiopia existed LONG before Solomon and Sheba as Abyssinia and before that as Kush. Western philosophy has corrupted our ability to think for ourselves. Haile Selassie was sent for us to be able to SEE, in our own image, the Legacy of our foremothers and forefathers that civilized the world. The western concept of a Leader is a cut-throat, down and dirty gets the job done type of person. Through his Imperial Majesty, we are taught that we are dignitaries of the Creator, and are governed by Natural Laws and know we are connected to the Creator as well. Through Marcus Garvey and Haile Selassie we are instilled with self-worth. Haile Selassie I can trace his genealogy thousands of years before Solomon and Sheba.

VII. ETHIOPIA AND ISLAM

Haile Selassie taught us that we are brothers with the Ethiopian, which means as brothers we come from the same root. One of the most neglected mentioned facts of Ethiopian history is that Empress Menen is a direct imperial descendant of Prophet Muhammad.

"The children and grandchildren of Haile Selassie are descended from the Prophet. A number of Ethiopian princes have been Muslim, and though this precluded their ascending the Imperial Throne it did not prevent them from ruling in their own dominions. Empress Menen, consort of Emperor Haile Selassie, bore a descent from the Prophet through her mother, Sehin, daughter of Negus Mikael (Muhammad Ali) of Wollo. Male descendants of the Prophet are Sharifs" (Abyssinia Forever n.d.).

The Lineage is based on the Mother, who was Ethiopian and Ethiopia, known in Ancient times as Kush, was the Holy land to the people of Ta'Maure misnomered Kemetians.

"The word Ke'metic is not the name of the people who resided in Ta'Maure', they were known as Ka'Mau. Ke'met is the name of the black soil (the soil is red because of the cataclysm that happened many years ago. read the Ebers Papyrus), not the "black people"(Kem'Nu is the term for black people) as we have erroneously have been taught. The name Ke'Met is a variation of Hek Ka Ptah, the name of the land is Ta'Maure, which has a dual meaning...(1) the Land of Amen Ra the actual longitude and latitude of the geographical land mass. (2) The physical human body"

-Mhtp Asaru Maat Ra Se Tepen Ra Ali El Bey, Asst G.S

"The people of Ethiopia and Trinidad and Tobago are joined in a massive and continuous effort to create for themselves a new and better way of life. They face many of the same problems."—H.I.M. Halie Selassie I

"Thousands of years ago, civilizations flourished in Africa which suffer not at all by comparison with those of other continents. In those centuries, Africans were politically free and economically independent. Their social patterns were their own and their cultures truly indigenous."- H.I.M. Halie Selassie I

VIII. Our Divine Prophet Noble Drew Ali

With us all citizens must proclaim their Nationality and we are teaching our people their Nationality and their Divine Creed that they may know that they are a part and a parcel of this said Government, and know that they are not Negroes, Colored Folks, Black People or Ethiopians, because these names were given to slaves by slave holders in 1779 and lasted until 1865 during the time of slavery, but this is a New Era of time now, and all men now must proclaim their free National Name to be recognized by the government in which they live and the nations of the earth, this is the reason why Allah, the Great God of the universe, *ordained Noble Drew Ali, The Prophet, to redeem his people from their sinful ways. The Moorish Americans are the descendants of the ancient Moabites whom inhabited the North Western and South Western shores of Africa.*—Act 6, Constitution and Bylaws of the Moorish Science Temple of America

"If you have Race Pride and Love your Race, join the Moorish Science Temple of America and become a part of this Divine Movement, then you will have power to redeem your race because you will know who you are, and who your forefathers were. Because where there is UNITY there is STRENGTH. "Together we stand, divided we Fall".

Come, good people, because I, the Prophet, sent to redeem this nation from mental slavery which you have now, I need every one of you who think that your condition can be better. This is a field open to strong men and women to uplift the nation and take your place in the affairs of men. If the Europeans and other nations are helping me, why not you? It is your problem. The Negro problem is being solved only as it can, and that is by the Moorish National

Divine Movement. If you have a nation you must have a FREE NATIONAL NAME in order to be RECOGNIZED by this nation as an American citizen. This is what was meant when it said, 'Seek ye first the kingdom of Heaven and all these things would be added unto you.'" –Noble Prophet Drew Ali

OUT OF DARKNESS

The First Atlantic System was the trade of *some* African slaves to mostly South American colonies of the Portuguese and Spanish empires. Keep in mind, when Christopher Columbus stumbled onto The Americas in 1492, thinking it was India, he met dark skinned natives with gold tipped spears. The Second Atlantic System was the trade of Moors who were prisoners of war, to mostly English, French and Dutch traders, taken from the Americas to the Caribbean. The main destinations of this phase of the Slave trade were the Caribbean colonies to fool us into thinking Slaves were *only* brought from Africa to America and those same slaves were taken to the Caribbean. European colonists initially practiced systems of both bonded labor and "Indian" slavery, enslaving many of the indigenous people, the Moors, of the so called New World. Indigenous peoples were the first used by Europeans as slaves in the Americas until a large numbers died from overwork and "Old World" diseases, which were in actuality New World diseases brought to the indigenous people by foreigner invaders. Africans replaced Indigenous people as the main population of slaves in the Americas. These Indigenous people were carried to the Caribbean as slaves and in most cases, such as on some of the Caribbean Islands, disease and warfare eliminated the Caribbean natives completely. These "Caribbean natives" were Moors of South America.

INTO MARVELOUS LIGHT

Prophet Noble Drew Ali Noble Drew Ali was born Timothy Drew on January 8th in 1886. In1913, he founded Moorish Science Temple of America in Newark,

New Jersey, but knew that Chicago would become the Moorish Mecca. The Moorish Science Temple was founded on teaching of the Moors used as the blueprint for Western Freemasonry. He taught Moors they were Scientist by Nature, and were natural persons with inalienable rights. He founded the Moorish Science Temple of America as a Divine and National Movement. Most people see this movement as an organization, a "Black" Masonic lodge or a temple for "Black Muslims" like the Nation of Islam, Nation of Gods and Earth or other sects of Islam. The Prophet taught that as Moorish Americans, we are descendants of Ancient Moabites, from Morocco, born here in the Americas. The Moorish Science Temple of America was founded to make Moors in America (incorrectly referred to as Negroes, Blacks, Coloreds, Afro-Americans, etc.) know their nationality and the religion of their Ancestors prior to the Trans-Atlantic and Sahara slave trades.

"The Negro is crying out for a Mohammad, a Prophet who will bring the Koran of economic and intelligent."—Messiah Marcus Garvey

Messiah Marcus Garvey prophesized the coming of Noble Drew Ali and was recognized by Drew Ali as his Forerunner. The Messiah said *"There shall be no solution to this race problem until you, yourselves, strike the blow for liberty."*

IX. WAS HAILE SELASSIE THE OPENER OR REVEALER OF THE 7 SEALS"?

And I saw a strong angel proclaiming with a loud voice

Who is worthy to open the book, and to loose the seals thereof?

And no man in heaven, or in earth,

Was able to open the book, neither to look thereon....

And one of the elders saith unto me, Weep not

Behold the Lion of the tribe of Judah, the Root of David, hath prevailed to open the book, and to loose the seven seals thereof.

Revelation 5:2-5

The book of Seven Seals is the Holy Koran of the Moorish Science Temple, Circle 7. The Holy Koran of the Moorish Science Temple of America is held to be a collection of knowledge kept secret by the Moslems of the East, now brought back to light by the Prophet. The Circle 7 Holy Koran is also published as the *Aquarian Gospel of Jesus the Christ* for the Masons of the world. (Dowling 1972)

The Aquarian Gospel of Jesus the Christ (*The Christ of the Piscean Age*) claims to be the true story of the life of Jesus, including the "lost" eighteen years silent in the New Testament. This text came to be known as the Holy Koran of the Moorish Science Temple of America, the title of which is never spelled Qur'an, it is referred to as the uniting of the Holy Koran of Mecca. Noble Drew Ali taught that Asiatics were Moslems, not MUSLIMS, and the Circle 7 is our Holy Book, with a red numeral seven surrounded by a blue circle broken into four segments.

The peoples of Asia, Africa, and the Pacific, as well as Latin Americans, and indigenous peoples of the Americas are all considered Asiatic in Moorish Science Temple teachings. Noble Drew Ali taught that Europeans represent the "Lower-self" (Satan), and a conscious Asiatic, Moorish American represented the Higher-self (God). Members of the Temple wear fezzes and turbans and add the suffixes Bey or El while Ali is not a name/ title Moors take. Ali is a given or exalted name. Our Moorish tribal names are titles that announce our Moorish heritage. Our fez is the national headdress of the Moors and represents the pinnacle of knowledge, wisdom and under, over and innerstanding. When you see the Fez, it says the wearer is a Moor, or that they are a student or Adept of Moorish Science, history and civilization. Freemasons also wear the fez, but based on their receiving 32 out of 360 degrees of knowledge; the Masonic tassel is pinned to the fez at 32 degrees, while the Moors' tassel swings 360 degrees.

Another very important thing about the fez:

The Fez is represented in Moorish Science as the Hex Alpha. The Hex Alpha is the Star of David, the Seal of Solomon and the symbol of the Moorish Fez. H.I.M representing the Star of David and adorning it on his person and Rases wearing the Star of David is a *spiritual* fez. The relation of H.I.M to the Solomonic dynasty isn't literal, it's the Secret Lesson that H.I.M belonged to the Ancient Moorish Empire that existed since the time of Hatshepsut, a.k.a. the Queen of Sheba, Ma'at-ka-Ra (Makare), Makeda in Ethiopian text Kebra Negast and Bilquis in the Quran, Ruler of Upper and Lower Kemet, when she visited the land of Punt. The women in Kemet carried the royal blood, not the males. The males in Kush carried the royal name. The creation of King Solomon, being the greater of the two powers between the meeting of Solomon And Sheba, was a ploy to introduce patriarchy by the European masons who could not conceptualize a wombman ruling over them as a matriarchy.

X. Moorish Scientific Standards

Our Flag is the Flag we inherited from our ancestors and which we use today. The star and its five (5) points stand for Man (the species, not the gender) or A.L.L.A.H. (an Arm, a Leg, a Leg, an Arm, and a Head). The five (5) points also stands for our Five (5) Principles of Love, Truth, Peace, Freedom and Justice. The way of life called ISLAM is an acronym I.S.L.A.M meaning I Self Law Am Master. Moorish Science unearths Aught from under the rubbish so MAN can perfect himself as a perfected stone in the temple of the Most High. The Moorish Scientist seeks to find "that which was lost" within himself, thus placing him on a path, journey or pilgrimage to Self Mastery and Spiritual Enlightenment. The seeking Moorish Scientist is called a traveler in search for the infinite and unchanging Truth, which is Aught, and Aught, which is Allah.

"...all men are one and equal to seek their own destiny; and to worship under their own vine and fig tree after the principles of the holy and divine laws of their forefathers."- (Noble Drew Ali, The Holy Koran of the Moorish Science Temple of America Circle 7 1928)

Divine Oral Statements and Prophesies
#4 *"I am going to stop the European from thinking and start you to thinking for your own good."* The Prophet is saying that with the European naturally being a thinker, since most have no soul, the Prophet will give us what we need to start thinking for ourselves instead of following the thoughts of the European.

#15 *"In the year 2000, the Moors will come into their own."*

#24 *"One day you will go to the store and there will be soldiers there with guns with bayonets on them and they will not let you enter. They will tell you move on."* Today with homeland security, martial law and the likes, we see these soldiers with guns but the bayonet isn't the blade nowadays it's the flashlight that replaced the bayonet.

#66 *"It will take you 50 years to find out what I brought you."* Moors were still mental slaves when the prophet introduced the Temple. He's saying it will take Moors a long time to really see his mission and vision for the Moorish Science Temple as a National and Divine, not a religious movement.

#107 *"There are going to be new Moors to come in with their eyes wide open, seeing and knowing, that are going to take you old moors and seat you in the back and carry out my Law."* Many Moors have failed the prophet through doing nothing to help uplift fallen humanity. Many moors saw the temple as a Church of some kind and have forgotten, neglected or created their own path with regard to following what the Prophet set forth. (Moorish Science Temple California, Inc. 2014)

The Prophet knew that Moors whom have never been introduced to the Temple will be, and will be so conscious that they will automatically see what the Prophet wanted us to do, and set about fulfilling what the Prophet established to bring us back into the fold of Government.

#139 *"If you are not careful your own brothers will try to sell you into slavery."*

#177 *"I will not teach you here, I will teach you on the Soul Plane."* Noble Drew Ali knows that in the mind is where the pineal gland rests. The pineal gland houses the soul of an individual with melanin and some non melanites. The Prophet comes to us in dreams and it is taught that if the Prophet does come to you in a dream, say nothing to him unless spoken to. This is where the real teachings are, in the realm of the soul.

#192 *"If your brother does something wrong to you, don't call him a nigger call him a dirty Moor."* The Prophet Noble Drew Ali was very aware that Melanin beings were and still are misnomers, and these misnomers delude to slavery. The Prophet is saying that we must identify even the ones of us that are unconscious and devilish as Moors, since we have our own ways of dealing with traitors of our Nation. If we identify them as niggers, we give up the right to discipline these dirty members of our society according to our Government.

What the emergence of the Prophet did was bring us back into the School of Thought we applied before Slavery. As Melanin beings and Moorish Americans that school of thought as a Religion is Universal. Meaning that our spirituality is based on Principles that govern the Universe and those Principles are manifested in Man through studying the Circle 7 Koran which is an activator of our Chakra system.

Chapter 12:

22. Behold a master (*Adept Chamber*) comes, and tells them of hidden wealth (*Kundalini energy*); that underneath the rocky coil of carnal things (base chakra) are treasures that no man can count. (*Spiritual enlightenment upon raising the Kundalini*)

23. That in the heart (chakra) the richest gems abound; that he who wills may open the door and find them all"   (Noble Drew Ali, The Holy Koran of the Moorish Science Temple of America Circle 7 1928)

Chapter 18:

39. "They saw the body of the Nazarene transmute. They saw it change from mortal (base Chakra) to immortal (Crown Chakra) and then it disappeared"- (Noble Drew Ali, The Holy Koran of the Moorish Science Temple of America Circle 7 1928)

"Sharif [Noble] Abdul Ali; in America he would be known as Noble Drew Ali. On his return to the United States in 1913 he had a dream in which he was ordered to found a movement to uplift fallen humanity by returning the nationality, divine creed and culture to persons of Moorish descent in the Western Hemisphere.

He organized the Moorish Science Temple along lines similar to Masonic lodges, with local temple branches and "Adept Chambers" teaching the esoteric wisdom derived from the secret circle of Eastern Sages, the Master Adepts of Moorish Science.- (Moors Gate : Bab al Magharbeh n.d.)

Moorish Elders through Moorish history teach about the Middle Passage story being a con to get the indigenous people of this land of North America, to disown their birthright. By abandonment of those rights through ignorance they are complicit in the theft of what's due to the Moors according to the Laws of Nations.

This is the ancient emblem of the Diocese of Freising, founded in the eighth century. The Moor's head is not rare in European heraldry. It still appears today in the arms of Sardinia and Corsica, as well as in the blazons of various

Popes Coat of Arms in the left corner of the shield is a Moor's head in natural colour with red

noble families. Italian heraldry, however, usually depicts the Moor wearing a diadem; a white band around his head instead of a crown, whereas in German heraldry the Moor is shown wearing a crown. The Moor's head found in the Bavarian tradition is known as the *caput Ethiopicum* or the Moor of Freising. In Christian tradition there are the Magi, also known as the Three Wise Men, The

Three Kings, or Kings from the East. The Magi depicted as the Moor was Zenone da Verona (about 300 - 371 or 300 - 380) and was either an early Christian Bishop or martyr. He is a saint in the Roman Catholic Church. His birth date is controversial but is placed sometime in the early 4th century in Mauritania near Algiers in North Africa, which tells us he truly was a Moor.

XII. MOORS AND THE NATION OF ISLAM

According to the history taught in the Nation Of Islam (N.O.I.), there is no connection to the Moorish Science Temple and Noble Drew Ali. David Ford El and Elijah Poole Bey were members of the M.S.T. of A. David Ford El had distinctive mixed parentage which allowed him at various times to claim to belong to several different races, usually African or Arab.

In November 1929, Ford El moved from Chicago to Detroit, Michigan and using the names Wallace D. Ford and Wallace D. Fard Muhammad. The faction he controlled he renamed the Allah Temple of Islam, established the University of Islam, formed a group of male security guards called the Fruit of Islam, and in 1930, he officially founded the N.O.I. One of Fard's first followers was Elijah Poole, who later changed his name to Elijah Muhammad. Elijah began preaching that Wallace Fard Muhammad was the Mahdi (prophesized redeemer of Islam) and even deified Fard as the True and Living God. Shortly before he departed Detroit for the last time, Fard conferred leadership of the Nation of Islam upon Elijah Muhammad. It is an undisputed fact that some Moors sold out the movement and joined the N.O.I. after the death of Noble Drew Ali in 1929. (Adwo El 2014).

With this overwhelming support, Fard laid the ideological foundation and Elijah built on it. What must be innerstood is that the N.O.I. was founded on the graves of Black Wall Street, the U.N.I.A., and the M.S.T. of A. It must be overstood that by late 1929 Black Wall Street, U.N.I.A. and M.S.T. of A. were neutralized and destabilized by the union states government corporation.

Claims Of The N.O.I.

- ❖ Asiatics were the non whites

- ❖ Islamism is attributed to W.D. Fard

- ❖ Elijah Muhammad began preaching that W.F. Muhammad was literally Allah in person as was emphasized in his book, *Message to the Blackman in America*.

"Allah (God) came to us from the Holy City Mecca, Arabia, in 1930. He used the name Wallace D. Fard, often signing it W.D. Fard. In the third year (1933), He signed His name W.F. Muhammad, which stands for Wallace Fard Muhammad." (Muhammad 2012)

- ❖ Up until 1935 (key date) N.O.I. members were issued and carried identification cards claiming Arabic names.

- ❖ Arabic names, or righteous names, was replaced with an "X" and the doctrine of Fard issuing righteous names to new members of the NOI upon his return from Mecca was forgotten

- ❖ Only privileged members received righteous names
  - o Cassius Clay- Muhammad Ali
  - o Malcolm X- El Hajj Malik Shabbaz
  - o Louis X- Louis Farrakhan.
  - o Elijah Poole Bey– Elijah Muhammad
  - o David Ford El– W.D Fard Muhammad

The Fruit of Islam, who were in actuality created from the Mufti Force in MST of A, wearing "so called" N.O.I. Fezzes at Elijah Muhammad's

The Truth: There would be no N.O.I. if first there wasn't Our Illustrious and Divine Prophet, Noble Drew Ali.

#1. "I brought you everything it takes to save a nation, now take it and save yourselves."

#207. "I have mended the broken wires and have connected them with Higher Powers"

(Moorish Science Temple California, Inc. 2014)

WORKS CITED

Abyssinia Forever. "Islam in Ethiopia." *Abyssinia Forever.* n.d. http://abyssinia2me.wordpress.com/history/.

Adwo El, Kudjo. *Noble Drew Ali Plenipotentiaries & The Negro Black and Coloured Addiction.* Edited by Tauheedah Sis. Najee-Ullah El. Redondo Beach, California: Califa Media, 2014.

Sovereignty. Performed by Amir Ali El. n.d.

Amir: Heru Ranesi El, G.S. *What Shall We Call Him?* Atlanta, GA: Moorish Science Temple of America, 2010.

Warnings from the Prophet Noble Drew Ali. Performed by Hakim Bey. n.d.

Black, H.C. *Black's Law Dictionary.* 4th. St.Paul, MN: West Publishing, 1891.

Dowling, Levi H. *The Aquarian Gospel of Jesus the Christ.* Camarillo, California: DeVorss & Company., 1972.

El Bey, Alim. *Precolonization of the Americas by African Moors.* n.d.

Moorish Science 101. Performed by C. Freeman El. n.d.

Garvey, Marcus. *Philosphies and Opinions of Marcus Garvey.* Edited by Amy J. Garvey. New York: Routledge, 1978.

Gorham Bey, E, and D. Rosser El. *Who Were The Negroes Before Slaves.* Hyattsville, MD: Moorish Pub, 2000.

Holy Day Service. Performed by Grand Body of the Prophet's Temple in Chicago. n.d.

Moors Conquest of Spain. Performed by Kaba Hiawatha Kamene. n.d.

Science is Seen, Spirituality is Unseen. Performed by Kaba Hiawatha Kamene. n.d.

Kaplan, Sydney. *The Black Presence in the Era of the American Revolution 1770-1800.* New York: New York Graphic Society, 1973.

Love El, R. *Oral Statements and Prophesies of Prophet Noble Drew Ali.* n.d.

Martin, E. and Law, J., ed. *Oxford Dictionary of Law*. Oxford, UK: Oxford University, 2009.

McLetchie El, Kevin. *From Kushite to Kemetan Melanin Trails*. Toronto: Kevin McLetchie, 2011.

Moorish Science Temple California, Inc. "Hadiths & Prophesies of Noble Drew Ali." In *Califa Uhuru*, by Prophet Noble Drew Ali, edited by Tauheedah Sis. Najee-Ullah El. Redondo Beach, California: Califa Media, 2014.

Moors Gate : Bab al Magharbeh. n.d. http://moorsgate.com.

Muhammad, Elijah. *Message to the Blackman in America*. Chicago: Final Call Inc. Publication, 2012.

Noble Drew Ali, Prophet. *101 Koran Questions for Moorish Americans*. Chicago: Moorish Guide Publishing, 1928.

—. *The Holy Koran of the Moorish Science Temple of America Circle 7*. Chicago: Moorish Guide Publishing, 1928.

Rastafari, Amen. *Kushite to Kemetic Melanin Trails. Religion vs. Spirituality: Metaphysics and Inner Ventures ofAmen Rastafari*. Toronto: Knowledge Press, 2007.

Coronation--Visit to Jamiaca--Lion of Judah. Performed by Haile Selassie I. 1966.

Smith, T. Wilson. *The Slave in Canda: A Collection of the Nova Scotia Historical Society for the Years 1896-1898, Vol. X*. Halifax, N.S.: Nova Scotia Printing Company, 1899.

Constitutional Fold of Government. Directed by Taj Tarik Bey. Performed by Taj Tarik Bey. n.d.

—. *Moors of the Roundtable Civic Lessons*. New York: R.V. Bey Publications, 1996.

—. *Nigger Industries, I & II*. New York: R.V. Bey Publications, n.d.

Nigger Industry I & II. Performed by Taj Tarik Bey. 2007.

What Law Is, What Law Is Not. Performed by Taj Tarik Bey. 2007.

The Wizard of Oz. Directed by Norman Taurog. 1939.

U.S. Government. "King Alfred Plan." U.S. Federal Government, 1984.

Van Pelt, Carter. "Interview with Brother Mutabarka PART II: Out of the
     Wilderness." *400 Years Pages*. 1998.
     http://incolor.inetnebr.com/cvanpelt/muta2.html.

Walker, James W. St. G. *The Black Loyalists: The Search for a Promised Land in
     Nova Scotia and Sierra Leone 1783-1870* . Toronto: University of Toronto
     Press, Scholarly Publishing Division, 1993.

Winks, Robin W. *The Blacks in Canada: A History.* Montreal: Mcgill Queens Univ
     Pr; 2, 1997.

Yogis, John. *Canadian Law Dictionary* . Hauppauge NY: Barron's Educational
     Series, 1990.

INDEX

Other Titles from Califa Media Publishing ™

Moorish Children's Guide to History and Culture

Moorish Jewels: Emerald Ed

Moors in America

Moslem Girls' Training Guide a.k.a. The Sisters' Auxiliary Handbook

Nationality, the Order of the Day

Noble Drew Ali Plenipotentiaries

Official Proclamation of Real Moorish American Nationality

Well, Come to Klanada

Califa Uhuru Series

Vol. 1: Holy Koran of the Moorish Holy Temple of Science, Circle 7

Vol. 2: "I'm Going to Repeat Myself.": A Collection of Artifacts Authored by Noble Prophet Drew Ali and the M.S.T. of A.

Vol. 3: Mysteries of the Silent Brotherhood of the East a.ka. The Red Book, a.k.a. Sincerity

Vol. 4: Califa Uhuru; A Collection of Literature from the Moorish Science Temple of America

www.ingramcontent.com/pod-product-compliance
Lightning Source LLC
Chambersburg PA
CBHW031134020426
42333CB00012B/380